Huddle Up

Huddle Up

Anecdotes and Thoughts
Of a High School Coach
From 50 Years of Fun, Friends, Family, And Football

GEORGE W. JEFFERSON

To order additional copies of this book, contact:
Xlibris Corporation
1-888-795-4274
www.Xlibris.com
Orders@Xlibris.com
43861

Contents

Foreword 9

Acknowledgements 11

Why Would You Choose To Be A Coach? 14

Be Yourself 16

The Head Coach Is Not An Island 17

Leadership 101 18

Assistant Coaches 19

Building a Strong Relationship With The School Administration And Faculty 21

Financing The Program 23

Get Mom Involved 25

Dads 26

The Coach Should Be A "Man of Letters" 28

Respect Your Players 30

Keeping It Simple 32

Program Wins 34

Traditions 36

Some Simple, Unconventional Program Beliefs 38

Throw Away The Scales And Tape Measures 40

Heart, Loyalty, and Camaraderie 42

Loyalty 44

Camaraderie 46

Go First Class 48

Hold on to Those Great Memories 50

Dedication

To our Grandchildren who have brought so much joy to our lives. Danny, the most personable and delightful guy I ever knew. We miss you, Danny but know you are in a better place. Greg, our first grandchild and our hero. Brian, also a hero and a great friend. Stevie, beautiful singer and a great student. James, the world class sportsman, and Kathryn who makes the world around her smile.

Foreword

ON A MISERABLY hot July day in Kentucky in 1982 the Campbellsville High School coaching staff was marking the practice field in preparation for the opening day of football practice. The paint-marking machine was old, rusty and repeatedly clogged up, This required work stoppage and tedious cleaning so we could continue our marking. The string that we used as a guide to mark the lines would break or get tangled when we attempted to stretch it across the field. As the sweat poured and the frustration gained momentum we felt that the job would never end and free us from this drudgery. When the cursed paint machine stopped up for about the tenth time, I overheard my newly graduated secondary coach, Gene Newsome, mutter "I'm quittin' this so I can be a corporate executive, or something." We roared at that incongruity in comparison to the dirty work we were doing.

Gene Newsome became an outstanding coach, we are still friends and we continue to laugh at our early attempts to build the ultimate football program. We had a great deal of enthusiasm, but very little material and resources.

Many people picture the coaching profession as a glamorous, very visible undertaking where you run onto the field with the band blaring and the fans leaping to their feet to pay homage to your genius as a play caller. In reality, the preparation for that brief sprint to glory is a long, tough, and arduous journey that will test your organizational skills, your patience, and most of all your commitment to the young people with whom you are privileged to work

This handbook will attempt to outline some time proven methods, ideas, and techniques that we have found to be effective in 50 years of working with high school programs that included small rural schools, suburban schools, inner city schools, and even a private military school.

This handbook is not about X's and O's. It is about preparing your program for the best chance to win and it's about preparing your players for life, and it is about building an honest program, built on integrity that is a good reflection on you, your school and your community.

Acknowledgements

I HAVE BEEN extremely fortunate to have been exposed to some of the best coaches in the profession. They are listed below along with some of their very unique skills, ideas, and contributions to the coaching profession. I sincerely hope that I absorbed just a little knowledge from each of them.

1949 – Claude Stewart (Greenville, Ms) E.E. Bass Junior High School. Coach Stewart was my first coach. He was a little "fireball" who taught us to love the game.

1951-1953 Carl Maddox, Maxie Lambright, and Harry Rowell (Greenville,Ms High School). Coach Maddox was our head coach and he advanced to L.S.U and helped them win the 1958 National Championship. He was a tremendous organizer and a major influence to all of his players. Maxie Lambright was an offensive genius and later was Terry Bradshaws' head coach at Louisiana Tech. Coach Rowell was my line coach in high school. He was very patient and calm and the perfect compliment to the fiery Maddox.

1954 – Coach Jim Randall, Jimmy Bellipani, and JD Stonestreet were very enthusiastic, hard working coaches at Sunflower Junior College (now Mississippi Delta CC) They were masters at creating a tight-knit,family atmosphere on the squad.

1954 -1956 – Phil Dickens, Bob Hicks, Lou McCollough, and Wilbur Stevens made up most of the staff at the University of Wyoming. These guys played and coached at Tennessee under General Bob Neyland. They brought his style of coaching and playing to Laramie and we learned about fundamentals, fundamentals, and more fundamentals! They kept things very simple and depended on execution, discipline, and conditioning to win. Apparently it worked because we won the 1955 Sun Bowl over Texas Tech and followed that up with an undefeated season in 1956. There were only three undefeated teams in the country in 1956 and our coaches loved to point out the fact that 2 of the 3 unbeaten teams (Wyoming and Tennessee) ran the single wing offense!

After I finished my eligibility at Wyoming, I stayed in school and worked with the Cowboy freshman team during the 1957 season. Coach Dickens and his staff had moved on to The University of Indiana. Coach Dickens was replaced by Bob Devaney. The Wyoming job was Coach Devaneys' first head coaching position. Little did we know that we were working with a future legend. What a break it was to get a chance to work under a head coach who later won two National Championships at Nebraska and who is now in the College Football Hall of Fame! His staff taught us a much more refined game than we had known previously.

1958-2007 Bill Magginis, Errol Bisso, Bob Kies, Ken Paxton, John Cumiskey, Chuck Connor, Paul Langner, Marc Paglia, Butch Bennett, Dave Fryrear, and Jim Markham, are some of the coaches I worked with at Riverside Military Academy.

Riverside offers a unique challenge because of the nature of the school. We are a boarding school with a fairly heavy turnover from year to year. Our coaches do a terrific job of coping with that problem and each year challenges their ability to rebuild.

Wayne Lee and I coached together at two different schools (Anguilla and Belzoni) in Mississippi in 1959-1964. Wayne was the assistant football coach and the best head basketball coach I've ever seen. He took 5'6" players, taught them a *relentless* press and won many more games than he should have. We did it all at Anguilla and Belzoni including washing the uniforms, driving the team bus, and marking the fields.

Jerry Sullivan and Ralph Frazure worked with Wayne and I after we moved on to Belzoni in 1961. Jerry taught me about understanding kids' limitations and not expecting a player to do things he cannot do. Jerry would find out a players strengths and build on those strengths. He was fond of saying" Don't penalize someone for what they *can't* do,.rather find out what he *can* do and glorify him!" Jerry has been a Pastor at several South Mississippi Baptist churches since retiring from coaching. Those communities have been extremely fortunate to have him!

In 1965 Dave Fryrear, my old friend from Riverside Military Academy, called and we got back together and started a new program at Iroquois HS in Louisville, Kentucky. Dave also hired Joe Blankenship, Jim Jordan, Andy Anderson, and Ray Bell.

We worked together for 7 years as a staff and gradually became competitive in a really tough Louisville city league.

In 1972 Dave moved to the athletic directors' job, and I was named head coach at Iroquois. Steve Reed, Gene Johnson, Mike O'Brien, and Bob Humphries rounded out our staff. We had some success in three years with a few high points such as the first wins over Manual and Flaget.

In 1975 I accepted the offensive line coaching job at Manual with head coach Buddy Pfaadt. We had a great staff with Steve Bocko, Steve Haag, Jelly Green, and Ray Adams. We were an inner city school and Buddy Pfaadt was a master at getting everything out of those kids. He was tough, sincere, fair, and consistent and they responded!

In 1981-82 Dave Fryrear called again from his new position as superintendent of schools in Campbellsville, Ky. We moved to Campbellsville and thoroughly enjoyed working with Dave Payne, Gene Newsome, and others at Campbellesville. We put together 2 straight winning seasons which seemed to please the community. Our grandchildren Greg, Brian, and Danny lived in Campbellsville at that time and, of course, that was a big bonus! The oldest grandson, Greg, 9 at the time, was a great team manager for the Eagles. Our second grandson, Brian, was 7 at that time and returned a few years later to play defensive tackle at Campbellsville College. Both grandsons would serve their country in the Second Gulf War after college.

We returned to Riverside Military Academy in 1983 and I coached on the football staff and served as head track coach for nine years before becoming assistant to the principal.

We learn, grow, and develop from every exposure to talented
Colleagues

Why Would You Choose
To Be A Coach?

IT IS UNLIKELY that many young people begin their school experience wanting to prepare themselves to be a high school coach, but at a certain point some will encounter an individual who will so impress them with their enthusiasm, fairness, dynamics and leadership that they will be steered towards coaching as a profession. Later in your career that individual could be you, unknowingly encouraging a young person toward a coaching career.

My high school coach, Carl Maddox, was the most influential person in my life, other than my father ... and I have always measured my work by what I thought he would approve of. He left Greenville (Ms) High School to become offensive coordinator at LSU in 1955 and helped them capture the National Championship in 1958. His program at Greenville was a model of organization and efficiency, and his ideas were light years ahead of his time.

Coach Jim Randall at Mississippi Delta Junior College was, and still is, a legend in Mississippi. He had a tremendous impact on his players and colleagues. Coach Randall was quite a taskmaster who could not shed the fatherly, caring image that overshadowed the tough guy opinion he had of himself. His former players relish the rare opportunities we have to get together and tell "Coach Randall Stories."

My favorite story concerns Coach Randalls' great ability to convince opposing coaches that his team is weak and unable to compete, in an effort to get the other team overconfident. Coach was visiting with an opposing coach in the infield at the conference track meet one spring and he was really bemoaning his chances of winning even one game next fall. His audience was "Bull" Sullivan, another legendary "cry baby" among junior college coaches. Coach Randall said "Shoot, Bull, my backs are so slow I can out run 'em! Coach Sullivan answered "Jim, I ain't got a lineman over 200 pounds! The old coaches were really working each over when a bird flew over and deposited on Coach Randalls' totally bald head. Coach Randall didn't even look up as he said "See there, Bull, that blankety-blank bird *sings* to everybody else!

About a dozen of my teammates from Delta went into and stayed in the coaching profession. Undoubtedly Coach Randall's influence guided us into coaching. He taught us the value of genuinely caring for the young players on the squad.

Our coaches at The University Of Wyoming in the middle fifties taught us about hard work and the will to win. Coach Phil Dickens and line coach Bob Hicks were from the General Neyland/Tennessee old school and taught fundamentals, consistency, and toughness as the staples for winning.

These coaches influenced me to spend a half-century of my life in an important and honorable profession.

Perhaps your admiration for your coaches and teachers has guided you to become a coach. You, in turn, may impress some youngsters with your abilities, character, and determination so that they will decide to follow in your footsteps. Your players will remember most of the things you say long after you have forgotten what you said. Many years later they will quote you verbatim; so it is important to realize that their memories will be of positive things you said. There is a tendency to block out what we do not want to hear and retain the good stuff. There are times when a bad practice, drill, or game cannot be glossed over, but after you make the necessary corrections it is important to leave the field or meeting with something positive for your players to sleep on and remember.

Go into coaching for the right reasons.
Stay positive, and always be cognizant of the fact that
Your players are listening and absorbing things
You say and do

Be Yourself

D ARRELL ROYAL, THE Hall of Fame coach for many years at The University of Texas, said "If you are not yourself, you couldn't convince your players that Doris Day is a girl!"

Coach Royal was convinced that the most important skill a coach needed is the ability to sell his players on what they were doing. He felt that it did not really matter what offensive or defensive schemes you ran as long as you could make it match your material and you believed in what you were doing and sold it to your players. Coach Royal said "If you put in a fancy offense and defense but don't really believe in what you are doing, old Joe Coach from Hicksville will come to town running an old fashioned single wing offense and a seven diamond defense and whup your butt every time because his kids *believe!*"

We all admire great coaching personalities like Vince Lombardi and Bear Bryant, but there was only one Vince and only one Bear. We certainly want to learn from the great coaches but we would lose our credibility if we emulated them.

Young people will see through a phony presentation in a New York minute; so be yourself and your kids will respect you and respond. Lost credibility is difficult to regain from young people.

Believe in what you are doing and be yourself

The Head Coach Is Not
An Island

BUILDING A FOOTBALL program is an endeavor that requires the ultimate team effort. The sport itself epitomizes teamwork because of the large number of players who must be in synch. Even small schools will use upwards of thirty players in a single game and all thirty must be prepared to contribute when, and if, needed. Organization, structure, and consistency are essential throughout the organization to insure that the team operates as one unit.

The Head Coach is responsible for building an organization with clearly defined goals. He will be required to enlist the help of many different individuals and groups in order to reach those goals. The following is a discussion of some of the people who will be essential contributors to the program.

*The head coach is going to need a tremendous amount of help
from many areas, and this help will mostly be earned by the head coach's
willingness and ability to work with others*

Leadership 101

I N ORDER TO get as many as 100 people working together, there has to be rock hard leadership from the head coach.

Without question, the foundation for leadership is the willingness of the leader to set the example. If the policy is that everyone must be present and on time, then the leader needs to be the first one there and the last one to leave, every time! Every policy, rule, and direction must apply for the leadership or there will be grumbling and disenchantment with the rules.

Good leadership also requires these 3 components, *firmness, fairness, and consistency.*

A leader will tick people off sometimes when he is firm. So be it! Rules, policies, and decisions are based on what is best for the group. Being fair will require that the leader look at all options and possibly even make changes in a policy, if a change is the *right* thing to do.

Consistency is a tremendous factor in establishing and maintaining the morale of the group. Most of us will accept decisions that affect us, if we know that the leadership is consistent with his decisions.

The ability and the willingness to *communicate* effectively is the mark of a good leader. It does no good to have the best plan in the world unless that plan is shared with and implemented by the players and coaches. A great leader will have all members of the organization on the same page by openly communicating with all concerned.

Finally, a good leader will put the concerns, problems, and wishes of his subordinates first. When a player or assistant coach shares a problem with the head coach, the head coach should never vent his own personal frustrations. That would minimize the *players* problem. Listen and give his concern and your advice top priority.

A Great Leader is Firm, Fair, Consistent and Always Sets The Right Example

Assistant Coaches

THIS GROUP, PLAYERS not withstanding, is unquestionably one of the keys to a successful program. These are the *teachers* in the program, these are the men who will help plan the program and then carry out the plan. If the members of a staff have the attributes of character, good work ethic, and knowledge of the game, then the number of assistant coaches is not too important. It is extremely important that whatever number of coaches you have, they work together, are loyal, and have bought into the program. Most head coaches agree that they would rather have a cohesive small staff than a dozen guys who do not fully contribute and might become a distraction.

My staff and I were attending a coaching clinic in Cincinnati many years ago and a large group had assembled in the room of a very successful high school coach from the area. We all wanted to hear his ideas and policies. A very young and brash assistant coach began venting about his head coach's faults and how he disagreed with his methods, etc. The young coach finished and asked the old veteran what he would do about the situation. The coach glared at him and answered "The first thing I would do is fire you for your lack of loyalty, but since I can't do that I'm going to advise my friend how you talk behind his back and hopefully he will get rid of you!" Needless to say, the young man left the room quickly and did not last long in the coaching profession.

Loyalty tops the list of important attributes for assistant coaches but loyalty must be earned. A wise head coach will listen to his assistants, evaluate their ideas, and discuss those ideas before making major decisions.

Staff meetings prior to the season should be the time for staff bonding. These meetings should be structured so that every assistant coach feels that he is an important cog in the organization. The head coach is wise to include his assistant coaches in planning and decision making.

I was the offensive line coach for Dave Fryrear for 7 years at Iroquois High School in Louisville, Kentucky. Dave had a wonderful way of utilizing his staff and making us feel like equal contributors to the overall program. Dave might suddenly ask us questions in front of the squad. He would say "Coach Jefferson, how do you want this trap play blocked?" Of course, he knew how he wanted it blocked! . . . We had spent hours on blocking rules prior to the season. That was one of his ways of making his assistants look good to the squad. The result of his efforts was a hard working, extremely loyal staff.

Assistant coaches will spend a tremendous amount of time with small groups and they will develop a different kind of relationship with that group than will the head coach. That relationship will vary depending on the assistant's personality, the nature of the position he coaches, and the personality of the group. Ultimately the position coaches may have a a better handle on the squads mood and attitude than the head coach. By constantly sharing this information with the staff, practices and game plans can be better formulated.

Team Teaching and Active Learning are popular methodologies among educators, and these techniques are never more skillfully used than by a smoothly organized coaching staff. The *class* each day, begins with a full meeting of the squad to outline the goals for the day. They then break off into small groups for instruction from specialists, namely, the assistant coaches. The coaches will follow a carefully scripted plan, with specific goals for a period of 15 to 20 minutes before changing groups or activities. Coaches know that drills and instruction are more effective when they don not exceed their group's attention span. When the group work is done, all groups gather for team work under the direction of the head coach. After the team work is done, the head coach will review the day's productivity and outline goals for the next day.

A well organized, enthusiastic football practice is a great example of
team teaching *and* active learning

Building a Strong Relationship With The School Administration And Faculty

WE LIKENED COACHING to teaching in the preceding paragraph, and it is important that we consider ourselves primarily faculty members. The coaches' students are under the glare of a spotlight on Friday night. They perform in front of many people other than their parents, but the fact remains that the athletic program is listed as an *extra curricular* activity, which means that academics comes first.

The Principal and all of the teachers will be an athletic program's biggest fan and supporter if the program is deserving. A list of reasons for having their approval of the program would be endless. Coaches are wise to make sure their program works within the framework of the school's philosophy and vision. Most administrators and teachers enjoy supporting a winning program and will continue to do so as long as the program does not become an entity unto itself.

One of my professors in college gave us some invaluable advice about nurturing relationships when we joined a faculty and staff. He recommended that we work very closely with the school secretary, the custodians, the shop teachers, and the school nurse in addition to the teachers and administrators. The professor drew a laugh when he recommended that we stay away from the home economics department unless we wanted to weigh 500 pounds from eating pies and brownees.

Coaches who support other activities will be very much appreciated. The sponsors of other extra curricular activities will most certainly return that support.

Joe Glenn, the fine head football coach at the University of Wyoming, had his team form a pre-game tunnel for the marching band before the homecoming game in 2004. The team raised their headgears and cheered the band as they marched on. Coach Glenn, undoubtedly, gained friends for the football program from the band director, the band members, and the band parents.

Coaches should be highly visible during the school day for many reasons. Teachers usually appreciate the presence of the coaches in the hallways of the school. Coaches in the hallways can be a deterrent to boisterous behavior by athletes and other students. Good communication with the teachers and staff can also insure that the coaches are cognizant of the players' progress in class. A coach can be an invaluable counselor to a student who is having difficulty in class. The coach has the students ear many hours during pre practice, on the bus before and after game trips, and during other informal times. If the teacher-coach relationship is at its professional best, much progress can be made in the players' academic development.

Mingling with all students can also be a great recruiting tool. Many boys could be just waiting for a coach to invite them to try sports.

The relationship between the principal and the coach must be one of understanding, communication, and must focus on the direction of the program. The coach is wise to keep the Principal advised on all problems, functions, and directions of the program. Never let your Principal get "blindsided" by a problem within or without the program. It is important for the Coach and the Principal to communicate openly about who is responsible for what. The Coach decides who plays and who does not based on performance. All parental calls concerning that matter should be routed to the coach. On the other hand, the principal decides who plays or doesn't play according to grades and conduct. Neither party should cross the line into the other's responsibility without first discussing the issue.

Gain and nurture the support of faculty and administration

Financing The Program

UNFORTUNATELY, GATE RECEIPTS alone seldom provide enough funds to run a first class program. In my opinion, over scheduling and so called money games against larger more powerful programs, is an inexcusable and abominable practice. To expose young people to competition not commensurate with their own abilities in order to make money is a vicious and unfair practice. It is important for the coaches to be aware of this and be prepared to use their energy and ingenuity to raise money. There are many creative ways to supplement the athletic budget. One thing to keep in mind is that people want to know where the money is going. If you need to raise money for new track uniforms, let it be known what the money is for. If the patrons only know that it is going into a general fund they may lose interest.

Parents are always receptive to a plea for equipment that involves safety or their child's well being. They are not always that eager to finance "frills."

My principal at a small Mississippi school advised me to be careful about spending budget money on un-needed equipment unless I raised the money outside. He explained that we were a hard working farm community and our patrons would do anything to help but they would appreciate us being prudent. I needed some serious work done on the game field and it only took a suggestion to one of those farmers to get 4 or 5 tractors and all the equipment needed that following Saturday! It didn't cost the school a penny and we wound up with a great playing field.

If the dressing room needs a coat of paint, buy a paint brush and paint it! We even made our own weights. We poured concrete in a hoop cheese container, stuck them on an old rusty pipe and had ourselves a barbell. A hundred pounds is a hundred pounds whether it's concrete or stainless steel!

An old friend of mine, the Late Sam Karr was a legendary basketball coach in Eastern Kentucky. Sam was a big-time winner in an area where basketball is a big-time passion.

Sam needed more money in the coffer at his school and decided to bring in a troupe of washed up professional wrestlers to perform in the local high school gym. The cast was headed up by Tojo Yamamoto, an aging former world heavyweight champion. The feature event was billed as a match between Tojo and Coach Karr. This announcement brought the people out of every hill and hollow in the area. The gym was packed to the rafters and rocking an hour before the first match.

The excitement mounted as the preliminary events led up to the main event. Finally, Tojo climbed into the ring. Then the spotlight swung around to Coach Karr making his way down the aisle. The crowd exploded at the sight of their hero in wrestling tights.

As soon as the match started, Tojo grabbed Coach and slammed him to the canvas. When Sam could manage to talk, he said "Tojo, every one of those hillbillies in the bleachers packs a gun and if you hurt me you ain't gonna get out of here alive!"

Sam claimed that that was his finest fund raiser ever but declined any rematch with Tojo Yamamoto.

Get Mom Involved

I N 1981 AND 1982 I was head coach at Campbellsville (Ky) High School. One of my outstanding assistants was Dave Payne, who regularly introduced original ideas to improve our program. The mothers of our squad members were unusually interested in the program and seemed more than willing to help when needed. Dave suggested that we form a club called "Gridiron Moms." The ladies responded and proved to be as good as the already established men's "Touchdown Club" at getting things done and raising money for the program.

We began to hold classes for the Moms on basic football rules, etc. We held the classes on Monday night and ended the class with an abbreviated showing of Friday nights game film. The moms then came up with the idea of bringing food to the Thursday night walk through and we started having a picnic for players, coaches, and cheerleaders following the practice session. The only problem we had was "holding the Mom's back" and convincing them to not serve too much heavy food on the night before the game! We carried this idea over to our various athletic banquets, and the Moms provided "pot luck" meals for the banquets. If you want good food, just have a group of ladies competing for compliments on their favorite dishes!

We felt that we strengthened our team bond through these activities. By including the parents in a family type atmosphere, we would promote unity and cohesiveness that would carry over to the field of play.

Dads

T EAM DADS CAN be a different story. Most of the Dads probably played high school football themselves and have a good fundamental idea of the game. Dads also have the "advantage" of listening to *endless* narration by the TV game experts and their breakdown and second guessing of every play. Sometimes this can influence Dads' thinking and he might just think your Quarterback can, or should, do the same things Peyton Manning does on TV! Sometimes it is very difficult for a Dad to accept the fact that his son must "play within" himself until he is prepared enough to move into the world of Peyton Manning!

It is important for the Dads to feel that they are a big part of the program, *up to a point!* We had a players' father at Iroquois High School in Louisville,Ky, in 1973 who enjoyed visiting in the coaches office after practice *every* day. His son was just *on* the squad, he was not a talented boy at all, but he worked hard and contributed in practice. The Dad didn't try to interfere at all; apparently he just liked hanging out with us!

One night after a poor practice, we wanted to get right to work and sort out the problems we had just had on the field, and we really did not have time for a visitor. The Dad made himself even more unwelcome by blurting out "Coach, you need to get rid of one of your guards because he is a troublemaker." I could not believe my ears; he had never interfered like that before. I lost my temper and ran him out of the office and told him not to come back! I walked back into the dressing room to cool off. When I returned, the coaches were laughing hysterically . . . . They had invited the Dad back in and he explained that he was talking about one of the game night *security* guards, not one of our linemen. The security guard had been overstepping his authority and pushing kids around in the parking lot! I quickly apologized to the Dad and made sure the security company was informed that they had a problem guy.

If communication between you and the parents is open and shared; many problems will be avoided. The coach is going to be questioned by parents who believe that their son is not getting enough playing time or is not playing the right position. These questions can easily be handled by answering truthfully that he needs more work, he needs more experience, etc.

Always be Up Front and Honest with Parents
But
Any comments to parents must be devoid of references to lack of character, courage, or any other perceived personal faults

The Coach Should Be
A "Man of Letters"

THE COACH SHOULD be a "man of letters" and stay in constant touch with the parents. Most parents will treasure a complimentary note about their son, and their appreciation can strengthen that "Partnership with Parents" It does not take much time to send out a note, either a form letter, or a personnel letter. Tell the parents that the coaching staff appreciates the young man's effort and dedication to the program. Tell them that he had a great day of practice. If he demonstrates a great attitude and work ethic, give the parents credit for instilling those traits.

Most athletes will also appreciate a note from the coach during "down time" such as summer break.

Rocky Lanz was a freshman at Riverside Military Academy in 1987 and he got our attention as a track athlete who quietly went about his training with great determination. Our 4 by 400 relay team that spring was very strong and we felt that we had an excellent opportunity to win the Riverside Invitational Championship. One of our relay team members pulled a muscle in the 200 meter race and had to be replaced. We decided to put the freshman, Lanz, in the open spot. Just before the race started, a torrential rain started falling and the conditions were horrible. I will never forget the freshman's effort in that race. Rocky ran his heart out! We didn't win but we found a winner who continued to progress in football, wrestling, and track. Rocky had a tremendous career during the rest of his time at Riverside.

After high school, Lanz went on to finish college, made the United States power lifting team, and then competed for the United States bobsled team.

I did not hear from Rocky for ten years after graduation. One day he walked in my office and began filling me in on his life and career. Then he pulled out a tattered piece of legal paper and told me it was a note I had sent him one summer when he was still at Riverside. It was just a reminder to stay in shape and some encouragement to set high goals for himself. Then he told me that, when things got tough over the years, he would pull the note out and depend on it to help keep him going. It was extremely gratifying to know that he appreciated that simple note that much. Yes, I cried when Rocky told me that!

Parents are not your enemies as some coaches believe. Parents will support you as long as they know that your work is in the best interest of their son. There is a lot of competition for young people's interest in this era including television, access to automobiles, part time jobs, etc. You will need a great deal of help from the parents in order to sell kids on playing football. A sincere note from you could turn the tide if players are disillusioned by the tough practices, by the bumps and bruises, or by the demanding pressure from the coaches. If coaches have sold the parents by presenting an honest program that promises to be beneficial to the young man, the coach will have an ally in the parents.

Create ownership of the program among your parents and athletes

Respect Your Players

I TOOK ON my first head coaching job when I was twenty three years old, one year out of college, and *without a clue!*

Coach Jim Randall, from Mississippi Delta Junior College, drove over to observe one of my practices one day, and I really yielded to the pressure of having my old mentor watching me work.

Coach Randall, as I mentioned earlier, was very influential in my life, and for some reason, which I can only attribute to my ignorance and youth, I thought he had come to watch *me* conduct a football practice. Of course, he was there to recruit players and could have cared less about how I ran my practice!

After a terrible workout that had me berating players and having temper fits that were uncalled for, I walked over to Coach and started apologizing for my teams' poor performance, blaming *them* for their lack of desire and hustle, etc. Coach Randall interrupted me and said, "*You* are the problem! If you keep telling them how bad they are, they *will be bad!* After all, you are the coach and I imagine you want them to believe every thing you tell them".

Coach Randall then pointed out that I had appeared to be someone else, during the practice, because he never knew me to be that negative before. He reinforced Coach Royal's edict that you must *be yourself* in order to be believable.

Certainly you can not tolerate poor execution, performance, and effort, but corrections should not be made in a sarcastic, personal or whiny way like that rookie coach in Mississippi back in the sixties!

Several years later, in the middle seventies, I was working as the offensive line coach at Manual High School in Louisville, Ky with Head Coach Buddy Pfaadt. Manual is a storied school with a football tradition that dates back to 1893. It has two

National Championships and many State Championships on its resume. We were an inner city school and attracted some tough kids but once they bought into the program, their loyalty was unquestioned. Athletics was important to them and their enthusiasm made it extremely rewarding to work with them.

We had a young man on our squad named James "Applehead" Montgomery. James had picked up that nickname when he sold candy apples at Manual Stadium as a junior high student. The fact that James had shaved his head at a time when long hair and Afros were popular probably had something to do with the nickname, too!

James was somewhat inarticulate, poorly dressed, and continually subjected to ridicule from his peers. When he showed up for football practice as a sophomore, he found some relief from the verbal abuse but he still did not work very hard at his position on the offensive line. He was not at all comfortable with adults and never asked questions or spoke to us unless absolutely necessary.

One day, to my surprise, he asked "Coach Jeff, why don't the coaches call me *Applehead?* I answered "Because we've got too much respect for you . . . . Besides, we can't depend on somebody who accepts a name like *Applehead* to be mature enough to block anybody and contribute to this team!" Coach Pfaadt overheard the exchange and told the squad to knock off "the *stupid* nicknames!" When Buddy Pfaadt told our squad to stop doing something, they stopped doing it! He was a tremendous disciplinarian and his order pretty much eliminated any more damaging trash talk directed at team members. James Montgomery had never been told that he was *respected,* and it seemed to have a positive effect on him We noticed an amazing difference in his confidence and attention to detail from that point. He proceeded to learn *everyone's* assignments, he improved his film study, and the teachers commented on his class work and attitude in class. We noticed renewed respect for James from his teammates as his level of performance improved when he stopped trying to entertain them with silly, self-deprecating actions. He finally realized that his "friends" were laughing *at him* not *with him;* so he set about to build a more positive image of himself.

This all sounds too simplistic and syrupy, but we learned that if sarcasm and "put downs" are demeaning to a young man's self esteem, they can affect his progress in a negative way.

James Montgomery's transformation from the team "clown" to one of our most effective leaders was very rewarding to our staff.

Gaining the respect of peers and authority is a tremendous motivator

Keeping It Simple

WE COACHES LOVE to *talk* about keeping things simple. We have many sayings to that effect, like the K.I.S.S. method (Keep It Simple Stupid) "Less is More", etc., but we all fall into the trap of trying to do too much. I love to watch Peyton Manning dissect a defense with his calls at the line and flawless execution but I can't ask an inexperienced high school QB to do the same. It is a terrible mistake to ask a young player to do more than he can do. Let him play "within himself" and progress step-by-step. I am sure Manning got to his present level that way.

Most coaches feel that young players lose their aggressiveness if they are confused and overwhelmed by too much information. Imagine a high school sophomore experiencing for the first time a large crowd, an older opponent across from him, great expectations from his family and peers, and having to master a complicated offense and defense. Under these circumstances he might be inclined to "freeze" when the ball is snapped. Certainly, if he is sure of his assignments his confidence level could help him overcome the other obstacles.

Simple solutions to simple problems can also increase our effectiveness as coaches.

In 1962 a young man named Royce Kilpatrick moved to our town, Belzoni, Ms and reported for spring football practice. Royce was 6'2" 195 pounds and he could fly! He was a first cousin to Billy Cannon, the Heisman Trophy winner from L.S.U. The first time he shredded my first team defense, I immediately started thinking about travel plans to the State Championship game and then taking him to visit L.S.U., Notre Dame, and Southern Cal. He was that good!

Royce didn't like to block when he wasn't carrying the ball and I started "riding his back" about that. As a matter of fact I pushed him so far he decided to quit and move back to live with a relative in Louisiana.

One of my closest friends and my favorite "philosopher" was a grizzled, old coach named Bo Godfrey. We had been team mates and colleagues for many years. Bo didn't pull punches and if you wanted an honest, to the point, no spin answer . . . He was your guy!

When I bemoaned the fact, to my friend Bo, that I had run off my best prospect, he, of course, asked me "why"? My answer was a typically neophyte coach's answer. "He wouldn't block and if he is going to play for me he has to be a *complete* player." (I probably had read that in a book by some big time coach). Bo Godfrey's advice was a masterpiece of a *simple solution* to a *simple problem*. He said "You dumb ass, why didn't you give *him* the ball and let someone *else* block?

Never impede Your Talented Players, Build Around Them

Program Wins

MOST COACHES AGREE that teams defeat *themselves* more often than they are beaten by the other team. The margin for error is greatly reduced when a team's goal is to do a few things well rather than trying to do too many things. One of the most flattering things a coach can hear is that his wins are *program* wins. This praise means that the team wins because they execute and prepare well, not necessarily because they have superior athletes.

A well structured youth program is essential to building a winning high school team. The head coach then has the advantage of introducing his drills, offense, and defense to his future players. The youth coaches should be included in all pre season organizational meetings and be required to teach the varsity terminology and basic offense, defense, and kicking game.

A great example of a lasting and efficient program is North Hall High School in Gainesville, Georgia. Coach Bob Christmas and his staff have won State championships in two states by running a simple system with the emphasis on execution, ball control, and conditioning. His youth program is a model of organization that utilizes enthusiastic young coaches who follow Coach Christmases plan to a "T." North Hall is a contender every year, yet they very seldom have college prospects. North Hall is successful because of their feeder system, their organization, their dependence on execution, and discipline. Their senior leadership is a big part of their success and that leadership is at it's best during their pre-season weight lifting. They have a two month time period called "Men of Summer" The players are required to make 20 of 24 of the lifting sessions in order to be pictured on posters that are displayed in businesses in the area. The sessions are at 7 am, Monday through Friday and if a player is *one second* late he is charged one half of a day. It has been a tradition that the seniors go pick up any squad member who doesn't show up on time.

A sound program *can help keep a team competitive*
When there is a shortage of talent.

Traditions

I T SEEMS THAT the older we get, the more we treasure tradition. Those traditions, that we value so much have a great deal to do with kids accepting ownership of the program. Can you imagine a school changing their nickname and colors because a coach or principal didn't like them? A former University of Wyoming president attempted to have the cowboy/bucking horse decal removed from the football helmets. He felt that the symbol was "Inconsistent with the intellectual image of the University." Needless to say his suggestion infuriated a state that is totally identified by that symbol. Also, needless to say that individual is no longer president of The University of Wyoming. A new coach or administrator on the block is wise to buy into old traditions and go slowly in establishing too many new traditions. Some traditions are so deeply imbedded as an identifying factor of a school it becomes impossible to imagine anything else. The Texas Longhorn, Michigans helmet decal, and Notre Dames' fight song are known to everyone and are important rallying points for fans and players of those programs.

Many teams have rituals that may seem unusual to an outsider, but are valued by the members of a team. Clemson players rub a stone at the entrance to the stadium as they run onto the field. The Ole Miss team walks through "The Grove" an area where fans tailgate before a game and Texas A&M players gather in front of the student body after a loss to practice cheers. The idea is that they lost because the spirit wasn't there during the game.

Some coaches pass out decals for exceptional play for players to stick on their helmets. These decals are highly prized by these huge, mature, players who have been known to question the statisticians when they feel they deserved another star or symbol to add to their collection.

Strong traditions help build pride, strength, and ownership in an organization because the members of the organization appreciate that their traditions are unique to them.

Some Simple, Unconventional Program Beliefs

I HAVE ALWAYS been fascinated by coaches who build their programs around a very simple philosophy that they stick with year after year. They are usually successful because their players grow up in the system and develop the attitude that their plan is the only plan. Some times the things they do is very unconventional and therein lies the fascination. As discussed earlier, the team's *belief* in the program is most of the battle.

Coach Jim Randall from Mississippi Delta Junior College had a philosophy concerning punt returns that was very simple, unconventional, and very successful. He believed that *no* punt return was the *best* punt return.

Coach Randall felt that working on punt returns in practice was too dangerous because of the open field blocks. He also believed that most long punt returns were called back by illegal block penalties anyway.

Instead of working on returns Coach Randall spent a great deal of time on a package of 4 or 5 punt blocks. He put one safety back to field the punt. He felt that several things happened when you pressured the punter all the time. 1. The chance of a bad snap increased. 2. The kicking team's coverage was delayed 3. The punter might be pressured into a bad drop resulting in a shanked kick. 4. The scouting report would cause the opponent to spend an inordinate amount of time working on this part of the game plan.

Coach Randall felt that the punt block was one of the most devastating and demoralizing plays in football to an opponent. Coach Randall and his staff believed in this philosophy and used it for over 30 years. When a staff devotes that much effort into *any* phase of the game, they will excel in that phase of the game.

Many great coaches are identified by the things that they believe in so much that they continue to perfect that part of the game year after year. Coach Woody Hayes ran the same off-tackle play on the goal line for many years. His opponents *knew* what he was going to do, but could not stop him. Coach Hayes teams had developed such confidence in the play that his players did not *believe* that they could be stopped.

Bob Dunaway was a very successful coach from Vicksburg and Rolling Fork, Mississippi who ran 90% of his offense into *his* sideline. His reasoning was that he could see what was going on better than you because the playing fields in Mississippi have very high crowns for drainage and he could also get subs in faster because his huddle was closer to his bench. Of course he had the ability to run big plays back to the wide side when you overly adjusted and was very creative with that part of his offense.

An example of Coach Dunaway's *supreme* confidence in himself and his program occurred at an Ole Miss coaching clinic in 1961. Legendary Coach Johnny Vaught, of Ole Miss was the main speaker. Hundreds of high school coaches had registered for the clinic to hear Coach Vaught speak about "Developing the Sprint Out Quarterback." Ole Miss was coming off a National Championship season and they were in the midst of a run of All-American quarterbacks that included Ray Brown, Jake Gibbs, and Archie Manning.

All of our attention was riveted on this great coaches presentation when Bob Dunaway suddenly interrupted him and said "Coach, we don't do things that way at Rolling Fork!" He then proceeded to tell Coach Vaught and the rest of the audience how they did it at Rolling Fork. He wasn't really being disrespectful or rude, he just *believed* so strongly in what they did at his tiny school. Coach Dunaway felt comfortable comparing his Rolling Fork methods to Ole Miss methods.

These are a few examples of unconventional ideas from coaches who "think outside the box" and believe strongly in what they are doing. Young coaches benefit from observing other coaches methods but should not try to implement ideas just because the ideas worked for someone else. It is extremely important that a coach plans his program around the material available, the strengths and abilities of his staff, the type of community expectations, the school atmosphere, and his personnel beliefs. The most important consideration is the coach's commitment to whatever plan he has. Nothing destroys confidence among players as much as constant change. If a coach spends all of preseason practice working on his "unstoppable offense" and selling it to the team, then abandons everything because it didn't work in the first game, the players will doubt his commitment and wonder if he knows what he is doing.

Have a reason, for what you do, however unique,
believe in what you do, and follow through

Throw Away The Scales
And Tape Measures

IN 1962 HE was about 5'6" and 123 pounds. He reported for football practice in July at Belzoni, Ms. He was just another eager kid in this small town who decided to find out what all the excitement was about. After a few days his younger brother joined the team. Mike and Gene Lewis' family lived in a small farm house10 miles out in the country. Their only source of water was a hand pump in the front yard.

The coaches all drove their personal cars to the far reaches of the county each night after football practice, ferrying players home. Mike and Gene were on my route. Many nights Mrs. Lewis would meet my car with fresh vegetables for my family from her garden. Mr Lewis was usually working away from home as a pipeline welder. The boys' mother made many sacrifices so that her boys' could play football instead of working in the afternoon and weekends.

From that beginning, Mike and Gene were a *coaches dream!* They hustled all the time, they accepted coaching, and they were quiet leaders. Mike gradually grew up to 147 pounds but he played a lot bigger! His work in the classroom was just as outstanding, and he won many academic honors.

After high school Mike Lewis played junior college linebacker at 165 pounds, and he was a good one! He continued to astound us by going on to Rhodes College where he was elected defensive captain and was named All-Conference linebacker.

Mike followed college with a tour in the Air Force as a fighter pilot. After his service to his country, he graduated near the top of his class at Ole Miss Law School and became a respected lawyer in Mississippi. In the early 90's the country boy who was too small to play and too disadvantaged to succeed, became a world famous lawyer by spearheading the famous "People vs Big Tobacco" class action law suit.

Tom Lorocco wrestled at 126 pounds in his senior year at Riverside Military Academy. He was a wide receiver in football and just an average 400 meter runner on the track team. Nothing in his resume indicated that he could play football anywhere other than at the high school level.

Lorocco gained a little weight and decided to walk on at division 1-AA Georgia Southern. He gained almost a "cult figure" status on the Southern campus because of his enthusiasm and hustle on the special teams. He was always the first man down the field on kickoff and punt coverage. He was constantly "pumping" his team up on the sideline and always willing to play anywhere they needed him. Tom's jersey number became the biggest seller in the campus souvenir shop.

Tom Lorocco's high school coaches were thrilled to see him play and contribute to Georgia Southern's team in 3 *National Championship* games. They won 2 of 3!

Jerry Hill was one of Coach Bob Devaney's first recruits at Wyoming in 1957. He was a skinny kid from tiny Lingle, Wyoming. One of my duties as a student assistant coach was to take the freshman offensive team down to run the opponents plays against the varsity defense. I would show the freshman team the opponents plays on a card in the huddle. Hill was a tough kid who ran very hard, but usually he would run the wrong way or block the wrong guy. One day he was off track even more than usual, and when I yelled at him he came back with a classic excuse! He answered, "Coach, I played 6 man football in high school, and I don't know which one of those circles on the card is me!"

Jerry Hill became a huge star at Wyoming and then played 9 years for the Baltimore Colts. He is the second leading rusher in Colt history and scored the Colt's only touchdown in Super Bowl III.

Height and weight are just numbers
Accomplishments are the only measurements
That really matter

Heart, Loyalty, and Camaraderie

ALL ATHLETICS, ESPECIALLY football, involves a tremendous amount of emotion. The list of emotions involved in playing and coaching sports would be endless. We talk about heart, not as a part of the anatomy, but as part of our emotional mind set. It is the factor that triggers the upset wins, the unbelievable performances, and the instant heroes.

I recall a story about a little football player in a small New England college in the 50's. He was not a gifted kid and saw very little playing time. One Saturday morning the little guy showed up at the coaches office early and in a visibly shaken state of mind. He began to beg the head coach to start him in that afternoon's game. The coach told him that he didn't really deserve to start, that his performance in practice wasn't that good and his lack of size and speed was a handicap. The kid persisted and the coach finally agreed to let him in the game at some point.

Early in the second quarter the coach made good on his promise and sent the young man in the game. He immediately took charge of the game. He was all over the field, making tackles from sideline to sideline. He blocked a punt and scooped the ball up and scored. In the defensive huddle, he took the leadership role and inspired the rest of the team to play better than they could. The performance of this third string player astounded the coach and after the game he pulled him aside. The coach said "Son, I have never seen anyone play that far above their ability. You were magnificent out there. How did you do it?"

The boy answered, "Thank you, Coach, for giving me the chance!" He continued, "Coach, you knew my Dad was blind, didn't you?" The coach answered "Yes, I've seen you walking with him on campus many times."

The boy looked up and said "Coach, my Dad died last night . . . . and today was the first time he ever *saw* me play.

Incredible Performances Sometimes Result From Inward Motivation

Loyalty

L OYALTY IS ANOTHER emotional factor that strengthens an individual and a team. Professional athletes are strongly criticized for their lack of loyalty when they switch teams for stronger contracts. That is just a fact of life, however they usually show a great deal of loyalty to their team mates while they are with a team. Being professionals, they realize that team success is what guides everyones success. On a lower level, loyalty to the high school or college team becomes more natural. Most boys will grow up and play for their home town team and will have developed heroes from that team. We usually can't imagine playing for anyone else, so loyalty is a given.

There are two gentlemen, Errol Bisso and Chris Lancaster, in my experience who epitomize the trait of loyalty. These two men have combined for over a half century of service to one school. As the saying goes, If you look up the word *Loyalty* in the dictionary their picture should be next to the definition.

Coach Errol Bisso was a sophomore lineman at Riverside Military Academy when I started my career there in 1958. He had entered Riverside in the 8th grade and quickly made a name for himself as a cadet leader. Errol played in the 1961 High School All-American Game and was signed by one of the coaches, Horace McCool, to play at Delta State University. After a fine career at Delta State, he did his graduate work and then returned to Riverside as assistant coach.

Coach Bisso has served Riverside as a student-athlete, a high ranking cadet officer, assistant football, basketball, baseball, and track coach. He has been head coach in football, track, and wrestling. Coach Bissos wrestling coaching career is nothing short of phenomenal! He guided Riverside's wrestling program to 406 wins, his teams won 3 state championships, he is a member of The National Wrestling Coaches Hall of

Fame. Coach Bisso is also a member of the North Georgia Sports Hall of Fame, and The Riverside Military Academy Hall of Fame.

All of the honors garnered by Errol Bisso pale in comparison to the influence he has had on literally thousands of Cadets since 1955. When a former cadet returns to visit the campus, his first question is "Where's Coach?" He is known as a tough taskmaster who gave his boys every advantage to succeed by insisting on honesty, integrity, and no shortcuts.

Coach Bisso's lovely wife, Barbara, has been at his side since they met in college and is almost as well known as the coach. She has helped run hundreds of tournaments and employed the same strict, no nonsense approach to her job, while smiling all the way!

Chris Lancaster entered Riverside in 1979 as a 7th grader, and like Coach Bisso, exhibited unusual leadership skills from the beginning. As Chris developed as a football player, wrestler, and track athlete his enthusiasm infused the entire school. We saw first hand that enthusiasm is, indeed, *contagious*. Our athletic teams were winning in excess of 75% of all our contests, without really outstanding athletes. Lancaster developed and matured physically and played his senior year at 230 pounds. He was signed by Clemson as a long snapper but refused to accept a part time job and worked his way into the starting fullback roll. Chris became the best blocking back in the nation and proved it by registering 14 knockdowns against Penn State in the Gator Bowl.

During his college playing career and his 19 year college coaching career at Kentucky, Baylor, and McNeese State this young man continued and still continues to back and support his high school.

Chris Lancaster is now the Athletic Director and Head Football Coach at his beloved Riverside Military Academy. Coach Lancaster has come home!

Loyalty to your Organization is Absolutely Neccessary

Camaraderie

MOST PLAYERS AND coaches say that the thing they miss most about leaving the game is the loss of camaraderie. Team sports require that all members bond and contribute equally to achieve a common goal. This is true of any organization whether it be a business or a sports team. Businesses are now using retreats and other team bonding methods to create a team atmosphere and build comraderie.

In a course of a season a team might be on a "roller coaster" ride of wins, losses, and adversity. During this ride coaches and players will be tested to the limit, and how the team bonds and reacts will determine the final outcome.

The staff's family members become very important cogs in the organization and lifelong friendships are formed as a result of a group of people who are all striving for the same result. It is important that the head coach allows his assistants to have some quality time with their families. Equally as important is that the head coach respect his own families contribution of their time to his endeavors. A coach desperately needs his families support.

My beautiful wife, Cathy, has been to literally hundreds of junior high, JV, high school, and college games during our 50+ years together. She has sat in the rain, snow, and heat while we played or scouted opponents. She was even at Drew, Mississippi on a hot, steamy night in 1963 when we scouted a freshman QB named Archie Manning. We are now huge fans of Archie's son's, NFL stars Peyton and Eli, and Cathy likes to reminisce about seeing the very beginning of the Manning football journey in that little Mississippi town so long ago.

She supported our own son's careers all the way through. Our oldest son, Mike, was a fine QB at Iroquois High School in Louisville and, according to Cathy, never actually threw an incompletion because there was pass interference by the opponent every time Mike's pass wasn't caught. Cathy was a State Champion in tennis singles in Mississippi in 1953 so she has a good understanding of what it takes to win and succeed in sports. Her support, enthusiasm and sacrifice has carried me for a long time.

Our youngest son, Randy, is the ultimate fan. He is the best friend Ole Miss ever had and lives and dies with his alma mater. Randy spent a lot of time with me on the practice field when he was in elementary school. He loved to ride the team bus to and from games. One night on the bus, after a particularly disappointing loss, my third grader suddenly said, "Dad, you ain't much of a Coach, are you?" All I could say was "Son don't say *ain't!*" His grammar may have been flawed, but his assessment of my coaching skills was right on the money!

Go First Class

YOUR PLAYERS AND how they conduct themselves off the field are an extension of you, your program, their parents, and the school they represent. I have heard coaches say "How does a guy's appearance or conduct at a post-game meal affect winning or losing?" The answer to that is that it could affect winning or losing by the breakdown in discipline on the field that surely follows off the field problems. Retention and recruitment of players could also be affected if parents learn of poor off the field supervision.

"Trash talk" and taunting has become very popular in professional athletics despite some efforts by authorities to control it. That activity has *no* place in high school sports and should be forbidden by high school coaches.

My dislike for "trash talk" goes back to a Wyoming/Arizona game in 1955. I was in the game at single wing center and my best friend was playing guard next to me. My friend was a whip-leather tough kid named Frank Bonds, who is still tough enough to break horses at age 72 on his Cheyenne ranch. Arizona featured a huge, mean nose guard whom our coaches had been touting all week. They told us that he was the biggest, strongest, nastiest defensive lineman in the country. Since he would be lining up on me, I was naturally concerned about this situation and listened intently to the coaches. I, admittedly, wondered if I was up to this task.

We broke the huddle and lined up for our first play. The big guy lined up on me and started pawing the ground and making unintelligible, animal like noises. My *friend*, Frank, made the situation worse by saying "We're gonna run right over *you* Fat Boy!" Evidently the Arizona player was sensitive about his weight because he almost *killed* me when I snapped the ball. When I recovered, we went in the huddle and Frank and I discussed the fact that he was challenging a really *big* person who had lined up on *me*. Frank just said "Why don't you just get tough, Jefferson?" On the next play, the big man moved over and lined up on Frank . . . . You guessed it! Frank didn't say a word!

Every body loses when there is too much "trash talk." The Arizona player lost his temper . . . . Frank almost lost me as a friend . . . . and I lost a couple of teeth!

We read and hear endless coverage of professional, and even college athletes, having brushes with the law and other off the field problems. The big majority of college and professional athletes are outstanding individuals with integrity and high character, however some media outlets prefer to cover the dark side of the news so that our high school athletes are subjected to reports that glorify misbehavior off the field.

Most successful programs insist that players present the right image to the public. Dress codes, good behavior in public places, proper language, during the game and practice sessions, and a display of sportsmanship will always benefit the program. Certainly it will benefit recruiting. Parents rightfully feel that their son deserves a first class atmosphere. Another benefit is the appreciation of your program by your school administration and faculty. Nothing pleases a principal more than a call from a restaurant manager praising your team's behavior at the post game meal.

In 1961-1964 I was coaching at Belzoni, Ms in the Delta Valley Conference in Mississippi. It was an outstanding conference and progressive as well as competitive. The DVC presented a Sportsmanship Trophy each year. The standards for winning the trophy included behavior of the team on the field or court, the behavior of the fans, the hospitality of cheerleaders, and even the spirit of the community. This trophy was highly coveted by the school administrators who served as judges. They were not allowed to vote on their own school but rumor has it that there was some aggressive "politicking" going on at the end of the school year. Most of the schools launched campaigns which included written welcomes and banners by the cheerleaders to the visiting cheerleaders, letters of welcome by the Principals to visiting administrators, the athletic directors would personally meet the game officials when they arrived, and department heads would write a letter of welcome to their counterpart at the opposing school. Belzoni High School won that trophy in 1964. I didn't get a raise as a result but my Principal was very happy. A happy Principal can be almost as good as a pay raise.

Contrary to some beliefs good sportsmanship, in no way, lessens the degree of competitiveness on the field.

Hold on to Those Great Memories

SPORTS PROVIDE THE opportunity to collect memories that are dear to your heart, strengthens your friendships and builds loyalty. Most of our sports memories are positive ones. Who wants to remember losses, fumbles or missed tackles? We invariably talk about the victories and successes and the failures just keep getting dimmer and dimmer.

I can't write about memories without mentioning one that is particularly vivid to my wife and I. In 2005 our granddaughter, Stevie Jefferson, auditioned for the honor of singing the National Anthem at the 2003 Sun Bowl game between The University of Washington and Purdue University in El Paso, Texas. She was chosen to sing the anthem and we immediately made our travel plans from Georgia.

The El Paso Times newspaper ran a contest prior to the game inviting readers to write an essay entitled "My Most Memorable Sun Bowl Experience." I entered the contest, and won, by writing about the fact that I had played in the Sun Bowl 48 years ago as a member of the 1955 Wyoming Cowboy team. I wrote that we defeated Texas Tech in a come-from-behind thriller but that thrill did not compare to the one we had when Stevie won that audition. Her grandmother and I shed many tears and suffered many goose bumps as that clear, beautiful voice filled the desert air.

The memories didn't stop there. When we returned home from El Paso I called my high school English teacher, Nell Thomas, age 90 and told her that her weakest English student had won an essay contest over 50 years after his last class with her. When she recovered from the shock she asked me to send it to her to read. I declined that offer for fear of her grading the punctuation, content, and spelling. Nell Thomas would not have been as forgiving as the person who judged the essay in El Paso.

The End